CASTLE

Consultant:

Chris Gravett was born in Broadstairs, Kent, England. He studied medieval history at the University of London and spent a number of years as a curator at the British Museum. He is currently a senior curator at the Royal Armouries in the Tower of London. He is the author of a number of books and articles on knights and castles and has acted as consultant on several others. He was involved with the film *Braveheart* and was a consultant for the BBC on their series *Ivanhoe*.

Artist and Author:

Mark Bergin was born in Hastings, England, in 1961. He studied at Eastbourne College of Art and has specialized in historical reconstructions, aviation, and maritime subjects since 1983. He has been commissioned by aerospace companies and has illustrated a number of books on flight. He has illustrated many books in the prize-winning *Inside Story* series as well as **Space Shuttle** and **Wonders of the World** in the *Fast Forward* series.

Editors:

Stephen Haynes
Caroline Coleman

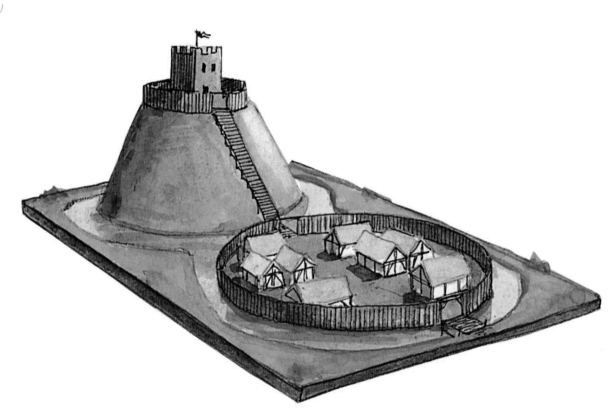

This edition first published in MMXV
by Book House

Distributed by Black Rabbit Books
P.O. Box 3263
Mankato
Minnesota MN 56002

Printed in the United States of America.
Printed on paper from sustainable forests.

Cataloging-in-Publication Data is available from the Library of Congress

HB ISBN: 978-1-905638-35-2
PB ISBN: 978-1-910184-25-7

CASTLE

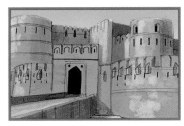

Written and illustrated by
MARK BERGIN

Created and designed by
DAVID SALARIYA

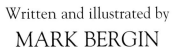

BOOK HOUSE

Contents

The Age of Castles

Throughout the Middle Ages, Europe was torn apart by wars and feuding. Castles were built for protection against enemy armies. They also protected those who worked on the castle lands and lived in the villages nearby. From 1050 to 1450, castle building was at its peak. Over time, castles became stronger and provided better protection, but none survived the invention of artillery.

King

Barons

Knights

Freemen

Peasants

▲ The nobility lived off the labor of the peasant classes under their control. In return for paying taxes, the peasants were able to take shelter within the castle walls in time of war. The nobility controlled everything.

▲ The king granted lands to those **barons** who swore allegiance to him. The barons then controlled the lands with the help of loyal knights. Freemen were the class between knights, and the masses of peasants who worked the land.

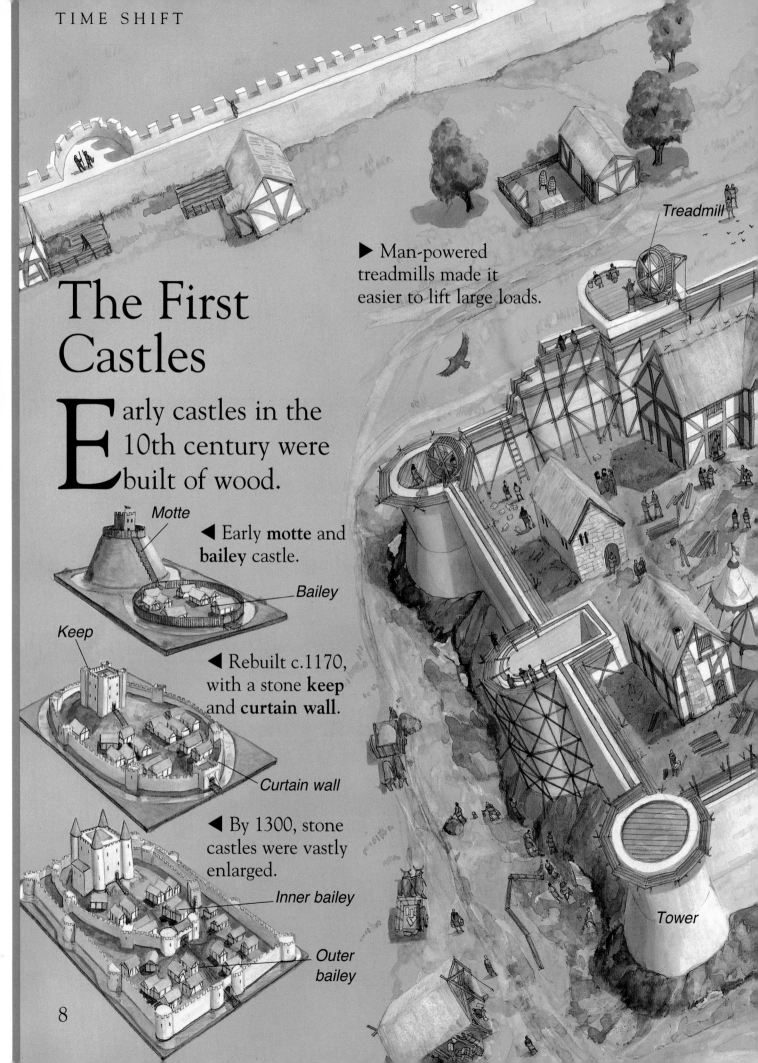

The First Castles

Early castles in the 10th century were built of wood.

◀ Man-powered treadmills made it easier to lift large loads.

Treadmill

Motte

◀ Early **motte** and **bailey** castle.

Bailey

Keep

◀ Rebuilt c.1170, with a stone **keep** and **curtain wall**.

Curtain wall

◀ By 1300, stone castles were vastly enlarged.

Inner bailey

Outer bailey

Tower

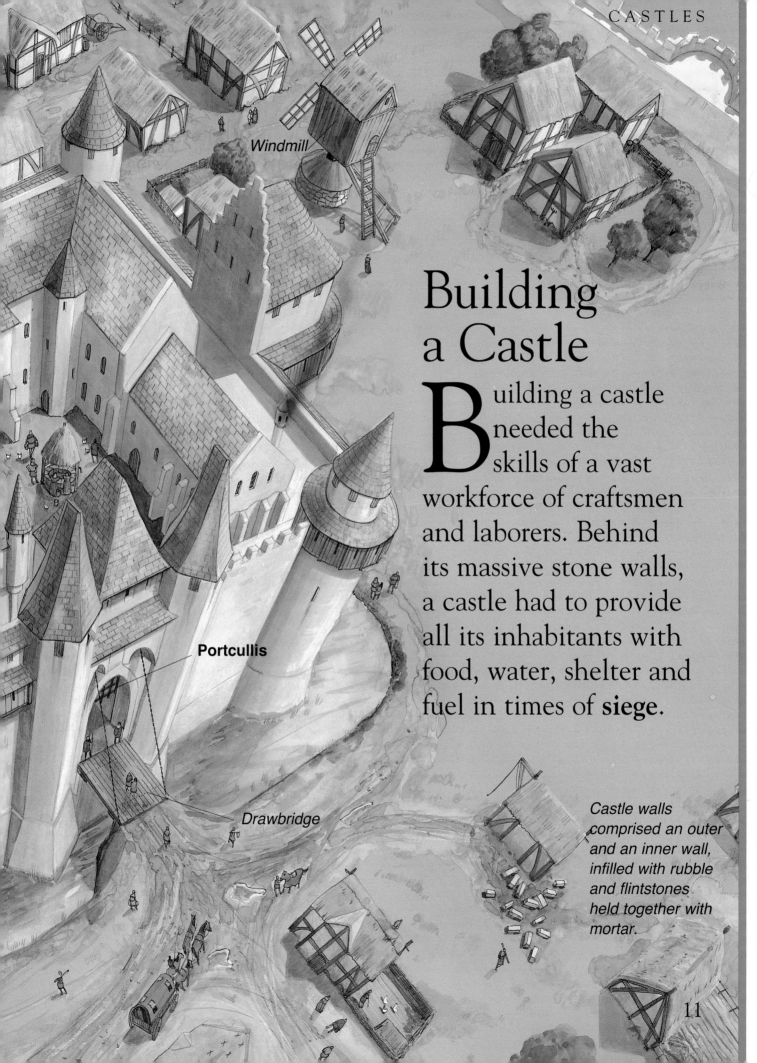

Windmill

Building a Castle

Building a castle needed the skills of a vast workforce of craftsmen and laborers. Behind its massive stone walls, a castle had to provide all its inhabitants with food, water, shelter and fuel in times of **siege**.

Portcullis

Drawbridge

Castle walls comprised an outer and an inner wall, infilled with rubble and flintstones held together with mortar.

11

Who's Who in the Castle

Jester Servant Lady's servant Bailiff Steward Page Cook Butler Pantler Falconer Knight Reeve

A castle was like a small town. The army of servants needed to run it, including a priest, blacksmith, wheelwright, carpenter and candlemaker, all lived within its walls. The marshal ran the **garrison**, clerks kept accounts, grooms tended horses, bailiffs collected rents and reeves managed the farms.

▶ Hunting provided meat for the table and larder.

Medieval nobles enjoyed riding, hunting and hawking.

▶ Noblewomen had to manage the castle when their lord was away.

▶ The church expected the noblility to give alms to the poor.

Baron or Lord

Lady

Marshal

Groom

Archer

A mounted archer could earn in two weeks what a farm laborer earned in a year.

▼ A suit of armor was very difficult to make. It had to fit its owner really well so he could fight in it.

▼ Large castles often had a jester to entertain the nobles and guests with singing and storytelling.

Armorer

Juggler

Jester

Minstrels

Everyday Life

The lord and lady lived in style, with lavish food and beautiful clothes. Their rooms had embroidered wall hangings, and curtains. Peasants enjoyed no such comfort and had to cook, eat, sleep, and wash in one room.

▶ A flag or **standard** raised on a tower showed that the lord was at home.

▼ The kitchen was usually in a separate building due to the risk of fires.

▼ The pantry and buttery (wine store) were nearby.

Servants and peasants would eat very plain food such as soups and stews.

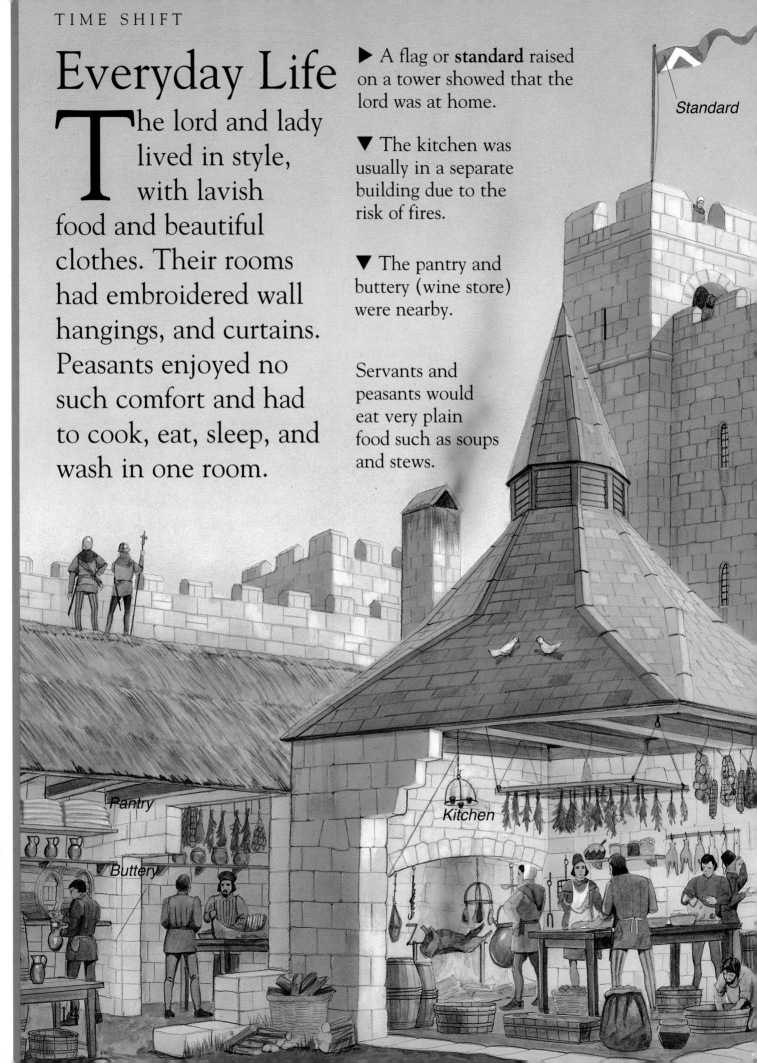

Standard

Pantry

Buttery

Kitchen

14

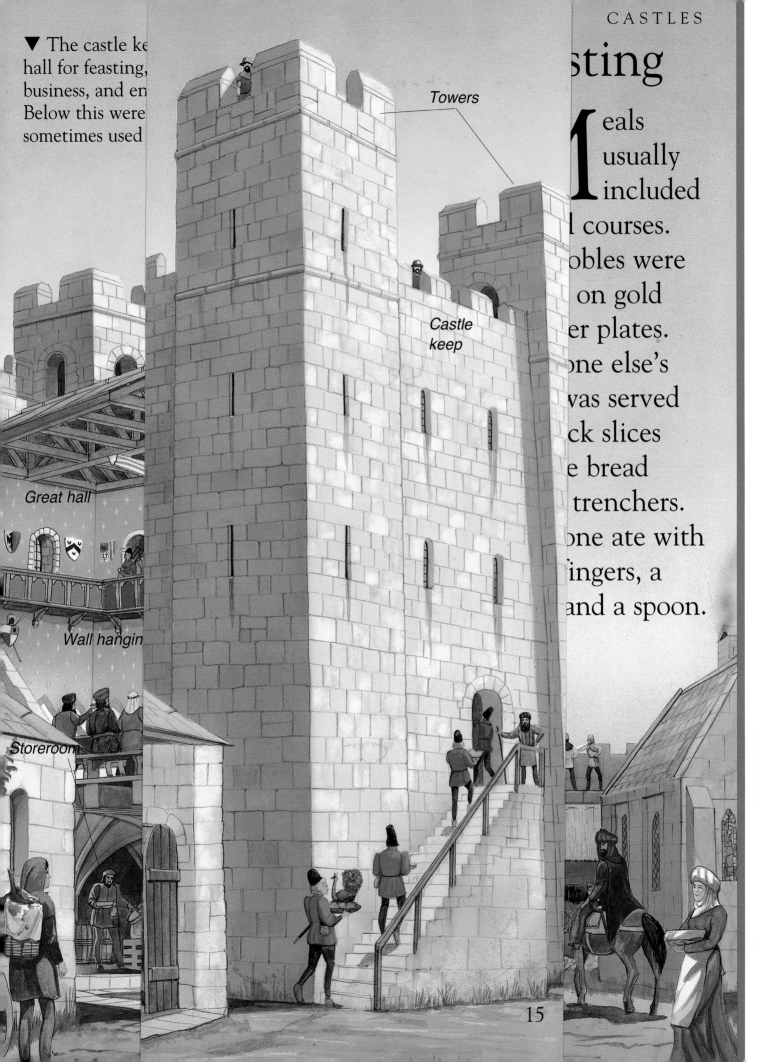

▼ The castle ke
hall for feasting,
business, and en
Below this were
sometimes used

Great hall

Wall hangin

Storeroom

Towers

Castle
keep

sting

eals usually
included
courses.
obles were
on gold
er plates.
ne else's
was served
ck slices
e bread
trenchers.
ne ate with
ingers, a
and a spoon.

15

Becoming a Knight

▼ A page had to run messages, wait tables, and learn the rules of polite society. He was also taught French and Latin.

Page

▲ Many boys aspired to become knights, but only wealthy boys were chosen.

A knight began his apprenticeship by working as a castle page, then as a **squire**: cleaning and caring for all his knight's armor and weapons and dressing him for battle. A squire with good skills in horsemanship and fighting could be a knight by the age of 21.

Squire

▶ A squire tying **plate armor** onto his knight's doublet (a padded undertunic).

Plate armor

Lance

Quintain

◀ Horsemanship and handling a **lance** was practised by riding at a rotating target called a **quintain**.

▼ Soldiers trained young squires in essential fighting skills, battle tactics and the rules of warfare.

Sword

Wooden shield

▼ A squire is knighted. At his dubbing ceremony, a sword tap on each shoulder marks his new status and he is presented with his sword and spurs.

Dubbing ceremony

Tournaments

Tournaments were huge social occasions where the knights displayed their strength and fighting skill to entertain the nobles.

Skilled knights took all the prizes.

Heraldic symbols

Surcoat

Shield with corner removed

Blunted sword

Lance tips

Basinet helmet

Knights on horseback were often maimed or killed in jousting contests. A tilt barrier was later introduced to prevent head-on collisions.

Pavilion

War Games

The highlight of the tournament was the joust, in which two knights rode at each other with lances.

▲ Knights also fought on foot, one on one. All tournament games were strictly managed by judges to stop any cheating.

23

Siege!

Until the 14th century and the invention of cannons, castles were almost impossible to destroy, so **sieges** were the best form of attack.

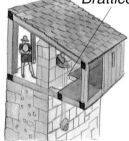

Brattices

◀ **Quicklime,** *stones, pitch, or boiling water were dropped on attackers from brattices overhanging the* **battlements***.*

▶ *Soldiers could hide behind the* **merlons** *and drop missiles through the* **machicolations** *onto the enemy.*

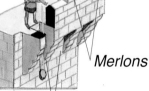

Merlons

Machicolations

◀ *The defenders shot arrows from narrow slits called arrow loops.*

▼ *Wooden shutters between the merlons gave added protection.*

Arrow loops

24

Merlons

Machicolations

Portcullis

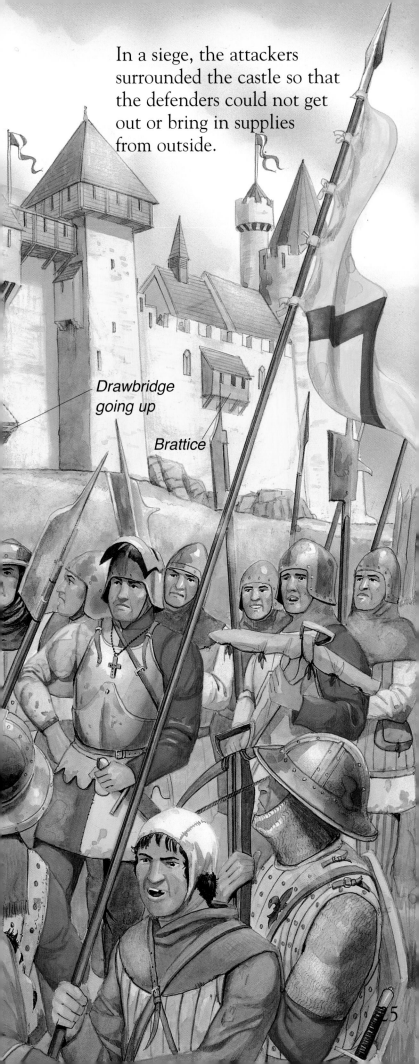

In a siege, the attackers surrounded the castle so that the defenders could not get out or bring in supplies from outside.

Drawbridge going up

Brattice

Ballista

26

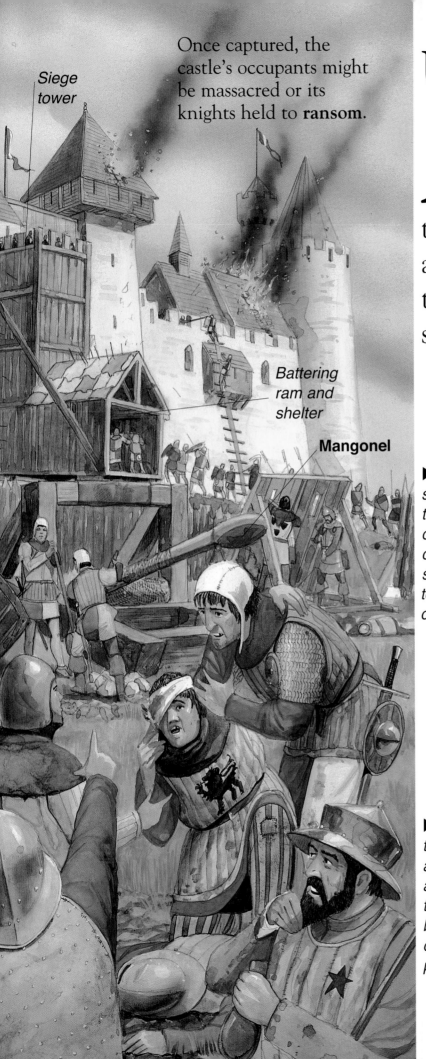

Siege tower

Once captured, the castle's occupants might be massacred or its knights held to **ransom**.

Battering ram and shelter

Mangonel

Under attack

Attackers would tunnel under the castle walls to make them collapse, and hurl heavy stones at them with their mighty siege machines.

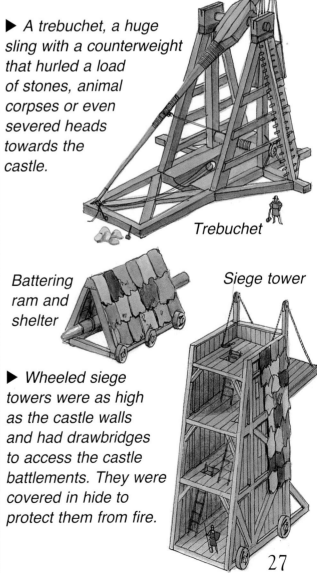

▶ A trebuchet, a huge sling with a counterweight that hurled a load of stones, animal corpses or even severed heads towards the castle.

Trebuchet

Battering ram and shelter

Siege tower

▶ Wheeled siege towers were as high as the castle walls and had drawbridges to access the castle battlements. They were covered in hide to protect them from fire.

27

Castles Around the World

Around the world, castles of many different architectural styles have served as fortified homes and as safe bases from which to govern. The 14th-century invention of the cannon undermined their military importance.

▲ This carving in Rome shows a fortified building called a *castrum*, the origin of the word "castle".

◀ Krak des Chevaliers in Syria, the most famous castle from the time of the **Crusades**.

▶ Himeji Castle, built in Japan in 1609, is covered in intricately carved and painted woodwork.

▶ The castle of Chillon was built on an island in Lake Geneva, Switzerland, to control shipping on the lake.

▼ The ornate castle of Ussé in France is an example of the 15th-century trend of building to impress.

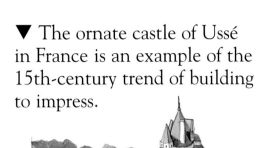

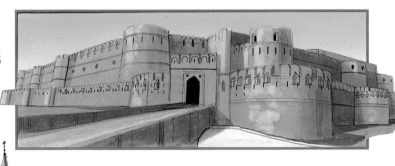

▲ The massive Indian fortress of Agra has 1.5 miles of surrounding walls that are 70 ft high.

◀ Neuschwanstein Castle, built for King Ludwig II of Bavaria, was completed in 1886. Shortly afterwards the king drowned himself.

▼ The British royal family still uses Windsor Castle in England, as a family home.

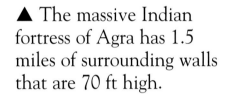

Today's tourists flock to castles around the world. Some are not true castles but were built for more decorative purposes by the new merchant classes.

Useful Words

Bailey
A castle courtyard.

Baron
A lord who held land for the king.

Battlements
Stonework on the top of castle walls that protected defending soldiers.

Crusades
A series of wars between Christian and Muslim armies.

Curtain wall
The outer wall of a castle complex.

Garrison
A castle's soldiers.

Gatehouse
A building guarding the entrance to a castle.

Heraldry
The system of symbols and colors identifying noble families.

Joust
A competition where knights tried to unhorse each other.

Keep
The central tower in a castle.

Lance
A long spear used by a knight on horseback.

Machicolations
Stonework on top of the castle walls from which objects could be dropped on attackers.

Mangonel
A very large catapult.

Merlons
The solid parts between the gaps on the top of the battlements.

Motte
A mound of earth on top of which a wooden tower would be built.

Plate armor
Armor made up of body–hugging sheets of metal plates.

Portcullis
A gate that could be raised and lowered at the entrance to a castle.

Quicklime
Powder that burned skin and clothing.

Quintain
A target for jousting practice.

Ransom
A sum of money demanded for the release of a captive.

Siege
The act of surrounding a castle to force its defenders to surrender.

Squire
Apprentice and personal servant to a knight.

Standard
The personal flag of a lord, king or other nobleman.

Surcoat
An outer garment worn by knights over their armor.

Tournaments
A series of contests consisting of mock fighting.

Castle Facts

Herstmonceux Castle in England had towers behind the drawbridge, which were equipped with artillery and had fighting platforms on top.

▼In the 13th century, Catalan kings rebuilt the 8th-century Arab fortress the Alcázar in Segovia, Spain.

In 1266, when King Edward I besieged Kenilworth Castle in England, it held out for a year because it had such impressive defences.

▶The stronghold of Dornie Castle in Scotland is a fine example of a fortified tower house with water on all sides, making it easy to defend.

▼The Pfalzgrafenstein, built by Emperor Louis IV in 1327, is known for its unusual hexagonal shape.

The Krak des Chevaliers in Syria had its own aqueduct and reservoir to provide water for its inhabitants.

The Palace of the Popes in France was built in 1370, when there were two rival popes.

Neuschwanstein Castle in Germany is a fantasy castle built in the 19th century.

It has a central-heating system, and the kitchen has hot and cold running water.

Borthwick Castle in Scotland is very strong, with over 13,000 tons (12,000 metric tons) of stone used for the outer facing, and the walls are over 13 ft (4 m) thick.

Although Himeji Castle in Japan is mostly built in wood, it is protected by stone walls and 20 gatehouses and its 8-story main keep is linked to three smaller keeps.

The Eagle Tower of Caernarfon Castle in Wales once had its own watergate and dock, providing an escape route to the sea and a way of bringing in supplies when under siege.

Index